THE MILITARY CREDIT BLUEPRINT

THE MILITARY CREDIT BLUEPRINT

THE STEP-BY-STEP GUIDE FOR MILITARY CREDIT REPAIR

CIERRA MICHELLE JONES, MBA

The Military Credit Blueprint:

The Step-By-Step Guide for Military Credit Repair / Cierra Michelle Jones, MBA

First Edition 2023

ISBN: 979-8-218-33941-8 (Paperback)

ISBN: 979-8-218-33942-5 (eBook)

Legal Disclaimer: This book is intended for informational purposes only. It contains the thoughts, opinions, and ideas of the author. It is sold with a clear understanding that the author is not providing legal advice to be used toward a specific set of facts. Please hire an attorney to address your needs if you require professional legal assistance. The author does not warrant the accuracy and completeness of the information herein. The author disclaims any responsibility or liability for the risk incurred as a result of the use/application of any of the contents of this book.

Scan the QR code below or visit.

militarycreditblueprint.com/bookfreebie to access free tools and resources.

I dedicate this book to my daughter Reagan, whose un-
conditional love inspired me to overcome some.
of the most challenging moments in my life.

To my dad, mom, and grandmother, thank you for always
praying for me, supporting my crazy dreams, and encour-
aging me to shine brighter.

To my team, thank you for holding me accountable
and helping me to finish strong.

This is just the beginning.

TABLE OF CONTENTS

"Money talks, but credit holds conversations."

PART I

BASIC TRAINING

CREDIT REPAIR BASICS

INTRODUCTION

Welcome to the Military Credit Blueprint. What started as a 300-page textbook about credit repair is now a blueprint exclusively for veterans on how to repair, rebuild, and restore their credit the legal way!

Now, you may be wondering how I managed to write a book on credit repair exclusively for military veterans. Well, that's easy. I served in the world's greatest Army – pardon my bias – for 15 years, and not only have I had my share of financial challenges, but I have witnessed other veterans struggle with their finances. Let's be honest: The military isn't the six-figure dream everyone thinks it is.

As veterans, we are trained to always be on the ready, whether it's preparing for a PCS, deployment, or what we all look forward to re-tirement. But despite countless hours of training or the hundreds of military regulations or Standard Operating Procedures that we have to memorize, financial education seems to be at the bottom of the military's Terminal Learning Objectives (TLOs).

I wanted the Military Credit Blueprint to be simple yet actionable. Instead of chapters, each section has been divided into steps, with easy-to-follow instructions on completing the credit repair process. While the blueprint was designed to be short and simple, it's packed with the information you need to get right to the point. This allows you to easily monitor – **and celebrate** – your progress.

If you're ready to learn how to design a no-fluff credit repair blueprint and get actionable steps to disputing negative accounts, such as collections, late payments, or even inquiries, then keep reading. If you want my personalized checklist on how to find account errors when reviewing your credit report, you're in the right place. The Military Credit Blueprint shows you how to do just that. If you want to know the ancient history of credit repair dating back to 1970, go to Google[1].

One of the leading causes of stress for military families is money. I created this blueprint for veterans to have one less thing to battle regarding their financial well-being.

Think of yourself as the financial architect of your future. You are one step closer to creating and leveraging better credit habits and designing a plan for financial success.

Let's begin.

---

[1] Google is a registered trademark of Google Inc

MY CREDIT REPAIR JOURNEY

W hen I realized how bad my credit was, I knew it was time to fix it, but I had no idea how or where to start. I'll never forget the day I went to buy a new car. My 1998 Mercury Tracer was on its last leg, and I needed a car, fast. I went to one of those dealerships on the side of the road – you know, the ones with the big red banner that promises, **"Bad Credit? No Problem: We can get you in a car."** Well, that day, they met their match.

One year earlier, I walked into the recruiter station and signed the dotted line to join the Army. When I went to buy my new car, I thought I could flex my veteran status to get approved. But I was in for a treat. By the time I left the dealership, the only thing I had to show for it was ten extra inquiries, a lower credit score than I started with - 438 to be exact - and a car that wouldn't last six months. But how exactly did I get here?

Back in the day, I made only $5.25/hour working in fast food. I had yet to learn what credit was, nor did I know how to manage my money. Honestly, I didn't even know how to use a credit card. That was until I got an offer to apply for one. I applied for a credit card from Capital One[2]® and instantly got approved for a credit card with a $500 credit limit. I was shocked. I got so excited that without even having the first card in hand, I applied for a SECOND card, and to my surprise, I got APPROVED. I had this crazy idea that credit cards were "free money. "But soon, I would realize the lie I was telling myself.

I didn't have many clothes and often wore the same clothes daily to school or work. If I did get something "new," it was off the rack of the local thrift shop. I decided to use my new credit cards and treat myself to a shopping spree, maxing out BOTH credit cards in under two hours. Once nothing was left, I went back to spending my penny-pinching fast-food paycheck and moved on as if nothing happened.

Until something did happen. After months of avoiding debt collectors, Capital One placed not one but TWO Civil judgments on my credit report. This means the accounts were not only charged off, but they also sued me for the debts. Capital One wanted their money back! And guess who didn't have it to give them? Me.

I was only 18 and still living with my parents. I had no clue what to do and was running out of options. So, I joined the Army, hoping to escape my poor financial decisions. This would be further from the truth.

---

[2] Capital One® is a registered trademark of Capital One Bank.

When I came back from Basic Training, I couldn't get approved for anything. I only had $-9.68 in my bank account and the clothes from my shopping spree. Since I couldn't get approved for an apartment with bad credit, I rented rooms from battle buddies or slept in my car. I would get denial after denial, and my credit mistakes would haunt me for the next five years. But the most embarrassing denial was being denied for a mortgage loan. After settling the judgments for my Capital One cards with the collection agency, in exchange for them agreeing to remove them, I thought all my bad credit mistakes had been erased. I got approved for an apartment and bought a new car but was still denied a mortgage loan.

Since I was applying for a new construction home loan, I signed the new sales contract, posted pictures of my "new house" on social media, and even wrote a check for $500 to secure the loan. But months later, the mortgage lender would tell me that underwriting denied my loan due to my poor credit. I was now homeless, lost my $500 earnest deposit, and wasted even more money using the lender's in-house credit repair company, which claimed they could fix my credit in just six months. Six months later, and nothing about my credit changed. I was back to the drawing board, more embarrassed than before. I sat in my car with my daughter, wondering where we would live.

I tried using other credit repair companies for credit repair, but I still didn't see results. So, like you, I searched the internet to learn how to fix my credit. I bought the "fix your credit" guides and even wrote and mailed letters with little to no results. I decided to dig deeper. I started researching the credit repair laws and used the information

I found to create a strategy. With some trial and error, I increased my credit score from 503 to 722. That's over 200 points!

Years later, I opened a credit repair company and helped thousands of veterans fix their credit and mindset about money. It's not just knowing how to improve your credit but realizing that you are creating opportunities for both you and your family to build generational wealth. When I first became a Board-Certified Credit Repair Consultant, I knew it was more than just mailing dispute letters. Of course, I'm not here to sell you a dream. This process took me years and a lot of rinse-and-repeat cycles. But I was determined to fix my credit to have financial stability, not just for me but for my daughter. I was finally approved to buy my dream home and closed on my new house in only thirty-one days.

Remember, this is not an overnight journey. There may be times during the process when you feel like giving up, but with time and patience, you'll get the desired results you're looking for. Before you close this guide, thinking it will take you ten years to fix your credit, let me preface it by saying I did the hard work so you wouldn't have to. What took me over ten years to learn can take you just a few hours of reading this guide and potentially six to nine months or less to implement.

I've been through the poor credit trenches, and I know it can become overwhelming. I know what it feels like to have to block debt collectors. I've had my car repossessed and even considered filing bankruptcy. But credit mistakes don't have to hold you back.

Congratulations in advance for taking the first step on your credit repair journey.

BOOTCAMP BASICS: WHAT IS CREDIT REPAIR?

B efore we get started, take a deep breath. As I mentioned, the credit repair journey is about trusting the process. You may think credit repair is simply disputing anything and everything off your credit reports, but it goes way beyond disputing. As defined by law, credit repair is the process of removing inaccurate, outdated, or unverifiable information from your credit reports. You have the right to have inaccurate data in your credit report corrected, and the credit reporting agencies have an obligation to ensure it's being reported correctly.

Credit repair is not a one-all-fix-all. Legal credit repair takes time and effort, but there are laws in place to protect you against harmful errors in your credit reports and harassment from creditors, such as the Fair Credit Reporting Act (FCRA)[3] and the Fair Debt Collection Practices Act (FDCPA)[4]. You have legal rights you probably don't know about, and collection agencies pray you never find out about.

The Credit Bureaus, or Credit Reporting Agencies, are not federal agencies. They are privately owned companies that do nothing more than keep records of your financial activity. A little-known fact is your credit score does not come directly from the credit bureaus but from various credit scoring algorithms that rate your financial history based on the information in your credit profile.

Ethical Credit Repair

Before you start, I want to remind you that credit repair is only legal and ethical when attempting to remove inaccurate, outdated, or unverifiable information. Under no circumstances do I endorse using these methods to remove accurate information from your credit file. These methods can and have been abused, and removing accurate information you know belongs to you is unethical and illegal, but I know you won't do that, right? RIGHT!

Even though you may be able to remove items from your report, removing them does not mean you do not owe them. If an inaccurate account is removed but still belongs to you, I recommend contacting the original creditors and requesting a settlement offer to reduce the chances of the account being sold to another collection agency, which may place it back on your credit reports.

---

[3] Read more about the FCRA on the Fair Trade Commission website:
https://www.ftc.gov/legal-library/browse/statutes/fair-credit-reporting-act
[4] Read more about the FDCPA on the Fair Trade Commission website:
https://www.ftc.gov/legal-library/browse/rules/fair-debt-collection-practices-act-text

YOUR LEGAL RIGHTS EXPLAINED

N ow, let's discuss the laws that protect you as a veteran, which will essentially ensure your credit report is free from errors. These laws also allow you to dispute and correct these errors. As mentioned, if these errors are not verified, timely, or accurately reported, the information must be removed from your credit report. **It's that simple.**

The Fair Credit Reporting Act or the FCRA, known as "the credit bible," ensures consumer credit reports **ONLY** report true and accurate information. The FCRA helps regulate what the credit bureaus are and are not allowed to do. However, according to the Federal Trade Commission, one in five Americans[5] still have multiple errors

---

[5] Read more about this on the Consumer Financial Protection Bureau Website: https://www.consumerfinance.gov/about-us/blog/common-errors-credit-report-and-how-get-them-fixed/

in their reports. The credit bureaus have 30 - 45 days to conduct investigations when you request them through the disputing process. If they fail to complete a timely investigation, the FCRA says they must remove the account.

Similarly, the Fair Debt Collection Practices Act (FDCPA) protects you against harassment from debt collectors. The FDCPA provides a list of unacceptable actions from debt collectors and creditors, the consequences for these actions, and when or if the companies violate your rights. With these two laws alone, you have the power to leverage your credit repair rights and fight back against shady debt collectors.

As a veteran, additional laws exist to protect you from predatory lenders, paying high-interest rates, and extra protection when you are deployed or serving on active duty. These laws are the Military Lending Act (MLA)[6] and the Servicemembers' Civil Relief Act (SCRA)[7].

I will discuss how these laws protect you in your credit repair journey. I will also review the statute of limitations and how this legal timeline is essential for repaying old debts.

The Fair Credit Reporting Act

The Fair Credit Reporting Act (FCRA) ensures the information provided by the credit bureaus and other credit reporting agencies (CRAs) is verifiable, accurate, and timely. The FCRA also protects the

---

[6] Read more about the MLA here: https://mla.dmdc.osd.mil/mla/#/home
[7] Read more about the SCRA here: https://scra.dmdc.osd.mil/scra/#/home

privacy of your information, ensuring lenders and banks don't access your credit reports without your permission.

Here's a summary of your rights under the FCRA:

- You have a right to be told if the information in your credit report has been used against you.
- You have a right to know what is on your credit report.
- You have the right to request your credit scores.
- You can dispute incomplete or inaccurate information on your credit report.
- When disputing items on your credit report, CRAs must correct or delete unverifiable, disputed information, usually within 30 days.
- CRAs cannot report outdated information. This includes negative accounts, which should not be on your credit report for more than seven years and 180 days from the initial delinquency date. The only exception is for bankruptcies, which can stay on your credit report for up to 10 years.
- Access to your credit reports is limited and should only be shared if a VALID need exists.
- You must give permission for your information to be shared with employers.
- You can opt out of "prescreened" credit and insurance offers you may have received based on information on your credit report.
- You can seek damages in state or federal court if your rights are violated.

- You are entitled to an annual, free credit report upon request.
- If you have been affected by identity theft, you can add a fraud alert to your credit report, preventing your credit profile from being compromised again.
- Active duty and activated veterans may also add an active-duty alert to their credit profiles, prompting lenders to verify their identity for all credit applications.

The Fair Debt Collection Practices Act

The Fair Debt Collection Practices Act protects consumers from illegal tactics by debt collectors. The FDCPA also ensures protection from abuse and harassment by debt collectors and regulates the Debt Collection Industry.

Here are some of your rights under the FDCPA:

- Debt collectors cannot ask you to pay excess interest, fees, or expenses not legally allowed.
- Debt collectors are not allowed to call you more than seven times within seven days of talking with you by phone.
- Debt collectors can't privately message you on social media after asking them to stop.
- Debt collectors cannot use obscene, profane, or abusive language.
- Debt collectors cannot call you before 8:00 a.m. or after 9:00 p.m.
- Debt collectors cannot use or threaten to use violence if you don't pay a debt.

- Debt collectors cannot discuss your debt with third parties unless you give them prior notice.
- Debt collectors can only inform the following people about your alleged debts:
  - Your attorney or the creditor's attorney;
  - The original creditor;
  - The Credit Bureaus or Credit Reporting Agencies, and
  - Your parent/guardian, if you are under 18.
- Debt collectors cannot repeatedly contact a third party to get your location information.
- Debt collectors cannot call you at work if you or your employer doesn't approve.
- Debt collectors must send a written debt validation notice within five days of the debt collector's initial communication.
- Debt collectors cannot ignore your written request to verify the alleged debt.
- Debt collectors cannot continue to collect on the debt before providing DEBT VERIFICATION.
- Debt collectors can't continue collection attempts after receiving a cease-and-desist communication notice.
- Debt collectors can't deposit a post-dated check early.
- Debt collectors are not allowed to reveal your debts to anyone, including placing information on mail correspondence.

Within their initial written communication, debt collectors are required to disclose the following:

- The name of the collection agency and their mailing address
- The name of the creditor you owe

- How much is owed, including interest and fees allowed by law.
- What to do to dispute the debt
- You have the right to request debt validation of the alleged debt within 30 days of receiving the initial debt collection letter.

The ultimate goal of debt collectors is to make you pay for alleged debts by any means necessary. You may not know that debt collection is a BILLION-dollar industry projected to grow over the next five years. This is why legal and illegal debt collectors persistently try to make money off your debts. FDCPA violations carry a fine of up to $1500. If you have proof that your rights were violated, you can file a claim in small claims court or contact a consumer law attorney in your state. Ensure the attorney specializes in consumer law and/or FDCPA violations. Most of these attorneys will work for free or receive compensation from the court settlement.

You should also keep **ALL** written correspondence you receive in the mail from a collection agency. Collection letters may contain violations, and if you decide to go to court, you or your attorney will need these letters as proof of a violation. Under the FDCPA, you have one year from the date of the alleged violation to sue the creditor and/or debt collector in small claims court. Depending on your state, small claims courts usually allow one hearing for you to present your case and prove the creditor and/or debt collector violated your rights.

You can also submit a complaint to federal agencies like the Federal Trade Commission (FTC) and the Consumer Financial Protection Bureau (CFPB). These agencies help consumers fight against debt collectors and settle financial matters with creditors. For more information on submitting complaints to these agencies, reference the bonus resources section of the guide.

Servicemembers' Civil Relief Act

The Servicemembers' Civil Relief Act provides financial and legal protections for active duty service members, including the National Guard, reserve members, and their families. SCRA rights may also be extended to anyone with a valid power of attorney for the servicemember. Some SCRA protections also apply to dependents.

Under the SCRA, servicemembers are granted the following protections:

- Reduced interest rates for credit cards;
- Postponing foreclosure;
- Deferring income taxes;
- Stopping evictions;
- Stopping default judgments;
- Delayed civil court matters;
- Protecting Small Business Owners;
- Termination of rental lease agreements;
- Termination of vehicle leases;
- Termination of cell phone service contracts;
- Life Insurance coverage;
- Suspension of Professional Liability Insurance; and
- Voting rights in your home state.

The SCRA requires that servicemembers be refunded the difference between any previous interest rates paid on an account minus the reduced interest rates while on active duty. For example, suppose you were initially paying an interest rate of 24% on a loan or credit card account and are currently on active duty once you notify the creditor of your active duty status. In that case, your interest rate will be reduced to 6%. Refunds also include renewal fees or any other applicable charges or fees paid.

Military Lending Act

The Military Lending Act (MLA) protects active duty, National Guard, and Reserve service members on orders for 30 days or more and certain military dependents from predatory lenders. The MLA limits the annual percentage rate for credit products or loans not to exceed 36%, including the costs associated with the loan, such as additional fees or the sale of credit products sold with the loan. This rate is known as the Military Annual Percentage Rate, or MAPR.

Below are examples of the types of accounts covered under the Military Lending Act:

- Payday loans, deposit advance products, tax refund anticipation loans, and vehicle title loans;
- Installment loans, not including installment loans expressly intended to finance the purchase of a vehicle or personal property, where credit is secured by the vehicle or personal property being purchased;
- Overdraft lines of credit, but not traditional overdraft services;
- Certain student loans and,

- Credit cards. (Note – credit card companies did not fall under the MLA until 2017. Creditors didn't have to comply with DoD's new rule until October 3, 2017).

Other MLA protections include:

- No mandatory waivers of your legal rights;
- No mandatory allotments, and
- No penalty for paying off accounts early.

Secured vehicle loans (using the vehicle as collateral to buy another) and secured mortgage loans (using the property as collateral to buy another) are **NOT** covered under the Military Lending Act. If the loan exceeds the 36% interest cap or violates other MLA provisions, creditors violating the MLA may be subject to penalties. There are some exceptions to the type of accounts that fall under the MLA, so always check with your finance company, JAG representative, and/or Consumer Credit Attorney for questions.

The Statute of Limitations

All debts, except federal debts, which include federal student loans, federal tax liens, etc., have a statute of limitation–or SOL. The statute of limitations is a timeline based on your state that regulates the timeframe for a creditor to legally sue you for a debt. The statute of limitations starts from the date of your last payment with the creditor. The SOL was established to protect you from debt collectors attempting to sue you for old debts, but it does NOT mean you still don't legally owe the debt.

If the debt falls outside the statute of limitations, you may no longer be sued for the alleged debt. Debt collectors or creditors may still report the debt to your credit reports if the last date of delinquency (the first time you were ever late or defaulted on the account) falls within the credit reporting timeframe, as outlined in the FCRA.

If a creditor or debt collector tries to sue you outside of the statute of limitations, you can sue them in court and possibly win if you can legally prove the statute of limitations expired. When disputing accounts, please remember that if the debt is still within the statute of limitations and you have not included it in a bankruptcy, you can still be sued, even if the account is removed from your credit reports.

The timeframe for debts to be reported on your credit reports is typically seven years and 180 days from the date of delinquency or account activity. Below is a chart[8] based on each state's debt reporting timeline, including types of accounts. These timeframes are subject to change at ANY TIME, so always research your state's SOL to ensure this information is current. If you PCS to another state, the statute of limitations is governed by your current state. Remember, the FCRA is a federal law and can override state debt collection laws.

---

[8] More on the Statute of Limitations: https://www.forbes.com/advisor/debt-relief/debt-relief-statute-of-limitations-debt-collection-by-state/

State	Oral Agree-ments	Written Contracts	Promissory Notes	Revolving Accounts
Alabama	6 years	6 years	6 years	3 years
Alaska	3 years	3 years	3 years	3 years
Arizona	3 years	6 years	6 years	3 years
Arkansas	3 years	5 years	5 years	5 years
California	2 years	4 years	4 years	4 years
Colorado	3 years	6 years	3 years	3 years
Connecticut	3 years	6 years	6 years	3 years
Delaware	3 years	3 years	3 years	3 years
Florida	4 years	5 years	4 years	4 years
Georgia	4 years	6 years	4 years	4 years
Hawaii	6 years	6 years	6 years	6 years
Idaho	4 years	5 years	5 years	4 years
Illinois	5 years	10 years	10 years	5 years
Indiana	6 years	10 years	6 years	6 years
Iowa	5 years	10 years	10 years	5 years
Kansas	3 years	5 years	5 years	5 years

Kentucky	5 years	10 years	10 years	5 years
Louisiana	10 years	10 years	10 years	3 years
Maine	6 years	6 years	20 years	6 years
Maryland	3 years	3 years	12 years	3 years
Massachusetts	6 years	6 years	6 years	6 years
Michigan	6 years	6 years	6 years	6 years
Minnesota	6 years	6 years	6 years	6 years
Mississippi	3 years	6 years	3 years	3 years
Missouri	5 years	10 years	3 years	5 years
Montana	5 years	8 years	5 years	5 years
Nebraska	4 years	5 years	5 years	4 years
Nevada	4 years	6 years	3 years	4 years
New Hampshire	3 years	3 years	6 years	3 years
New Jersey	6 years	6 years	6 years	6 years
New Mexico	4 years	6 years	4 years	4 years
New York	6 years	6 years	6 years	6 years
North Carolina	3 years	3 years	3 years	3 years

North Dakota	6 years	6 years	6 years	6 years
Ohio	6 years	8 years	6 years	6 years
Oklahoma	3 years	5 years	6 years	5 years
Oregon	6 years	6 years	6 years	6 years
Pennsylvania	4 years	4 years	4 years	4 years
Rhode Island	10 years	10 years	10 years	10 years
South Carolina	3 years	3 years	3 years	3 years
South Dakota	6 years	6 years	6 years	6 years
Tennessee	6 years	6 years	6 years	6 years
Texas	4 years	4 years	4 years	4 years
Utah	4 years	6 years	4 years	4 years
Vermont	6 years	6 years	14 years	6 years
Virginia	3 years	5 years	6 years	3 years
Washington	3 years	6 years	6 years	6 years
West Virginia	5 years	10 years	6 years	5 years
Wisconsin	6 years	6 years	10 years	6 years
Wyoming	8 years	10 years	10 years	6 years

Types of Legal Debt Agreements

Oral contracts, often called verbal agreements, are agreements where you agree to repay the money loaned to you (i.e., no written contract, "handshake agreement"). Remember, even though an oral contract is legal, it is difficult to prove in court, so these contracts are NOT recommended. Written contracts are when you agree to pay on a loan under the terms written in a document, signed by you and a debtor. Promissory notes are similar to a written contract. The key difference between a promissory note and a regular written contract is that the scheduled payments and interest on the loan are also included in the promissory note. A mortgage loan is an example of a promissory note. Revolving accounts are lines of credit with varying balances. The best example is a credit card account.

Credit Tip:
Credit Cards are ALWAYS considered open accounts, as established under the Truth-in-Lending Act.

Old debts, often called expired debts, fall outside the statute of limitations and the seven-year mark as governed by the FCRA. Old debts cannot be reinserted on your credit report as new debts. It's important to know that debt collection is still a legal business, so if a collection agency buys the debt, they legally have the right to collect on it, even if you do not have a contract with them. Collection agencies must also stop collection efforts if they cannot produce an original bill or signed contract from the original creditor. If they cannot collect on the debt, a debt collector will likely sell your debt to another collection agency. I'll cover how to dispute and settle collections in steps eight and nine.

CALCULATING YOUR CREDIT SCORES

What Is a Credit Score?

Your credit score is a numeric value assigned to your credit file, which rates your creditworthiness. This scoring system consists of a complex algorithm created by companies such as FICO and VantageScore. Contrary to popular belief, the scores from Credit Karma are not "fake" credit scores. Credit Karma uses VantageScore 3.0 for its free credit score application. Most credit scoring applications that give free access to your credit reports and scores use this model. VantageScore is the second most used scoring system after FICO.

Your credit reports are like fingerprints. Each credit bureau stores your information differently, so your credit reports and scores are not identical. Creditors must also pay credit reporting agencies to report your information. However, creditors are not required to report to the major credit bureaus. There is an exception for federal student loans that must be reported when the loans are dispersed.

VantageScores

Unlike FICO, VantageScore[9] forgives consumers for serious delinquencies during natural disasters. This algorithm also rewards "high quality" consumers for accounts that are paid off, like cars and mortgages. According to VantageScore, a high-quality consumer has a "perfect" credit history, meaning no late payments, high credit card balances, or public records. Vantage also excludes paid collections and minimizes the impact of authorized user piggybacking.

Credit Myth:

Creditors don't use credit karma, so those scores don't matter.

FACT: Some companies, like Synchrony Bank, use VantageScore credit scores when reviewing your credit applications. It's important to monitor this score as well as your FICO scores.

The Five Factors of FICO Scores

Your FICO score is calculated based on five factors. The two largest components of your FICO score are your payment history and credit card utilization. Making on-time payments, known as your payment history, is 35% of your FICO scores. But payment history isn't the only thing that can impact your scores. Your credit card utilization

---

[9] VantagSscore is a registered trademark of VantageScore Solutions, LLC

(or how much you spend on your credit cards compared to your limit) is 30% of your FICO score. These two factors alone make up 65% of your credit scores. If you've ever missed a payment by more than 30 days or maxed out your credit cards, more than likely, your credit score took a serious hit. The later your payments — whether 30, 60, 90, or 120 days — the lower your credit scores. Missing a payment by more than 90 days is equivalent to bankruptcy and can lower your credit scores by 200+ points.

It is important to keep a payment calendar of when your recurring payments are due to prevent your scores from dropping. Remember when I shared how I thought credit cards were free money? This was a painful lesson on not using my credit cards responsibly. And, like you, my first harsh lesson about payment history and credit card debt.

Speaking of credit cards, I'll dive into how to ensure you are using your credit cards responsibly. Let's say you have a credit card with a $5,000 limit and a balance of $1,000; this means you are using 20% of your total credit card limit. Ideally, you should only be using 5% to 10% of your overall credit limit, which, for this example, would be between $250 - $500. Using your credit cards responsibly shows credit card companies you can afford the monthly payments, which boosts your chances of getting higher credit limits.

Carrying a balance on your credit cards adds interest. The interest paid could range between $35 to $100 or more, depending on your annual percentage rate or APR. Get in the habit of paying your credit cards in full - or as close to 10% as possible, **BEFORE** your payment due date or statement closing date to avoid interest.

Your statement closing date and your payment due date are not the same. Your statement closing date is the date your billing cycle ends. Your payment due date, as you know, is the date that your credit card payment is due. Your due date is roughly 21 days after your statement date. Let's say you have a credit card with a $5,000 limit and use $1,000 of that limit. If your statement date is October 26th, the amount that will be reported to the credit bureaus based on your statement date is $1,000 unless this amount is paid in full before the statement date. You would ideally pay off your entire balance before your payment due date to prevent incurring interest.

Credit Myth:
Paying my credit card bill twice helps my score go up!
FACT: In most cases, creditors only report
your account balances once per month.

Making additional payments does lower your total balances, which can improve your credit scores. To expedite paying down credit cards, break payments down into biweekly payments instead of making a lump sum once a month.

Credit Age

Your credit age is calculated by averaging how long your credit accounts have been open. The longer you keep your credit accounts open, the better it is for your credit age, which is 15% of your FICO score. This is why prematurely closing credit cards is not recommended. If you need to close a credit card prematurely, only do so after having a backup card with a higher credit limit. Closing a credit card may temporarily lower your score, but you can build it by showing responsibility with your new card. If you do not use the card responsibly, it may be best to close it and reapply when you have more discipline.

Credit Mix

Your credit mix, or the types of accounts you have opened, is 10% of your FICO score. Ideally, the best credit mix is having a minimum of three revolving accounts, which include credit cards, and two installment accounts, which include car, mortgages, and student loans. If you already have three or more credit cards, keep your balances on existing cards low. Once you have established at least 24 months of positive history, you can apply for a more prestigious card with a higher limit, such as American Express[10].

Credit Inquiries

Credit inquiries make up 10% of your FICO score. Applying for new credit temporarily lowers your credit score and impacts your credit age. Even with credit experience, opening a new account can initially lower your scores, but building a positive payment history with your existing accounts can quickly help your scores increase. Inquiries are also scored under the new credit section of your credit reports. Credit inquiries stay on your credit reports for up to 25 months. Too many inquiries show lenders you may be credit shopping and can lower a good credit score.

---

[10] American Express is a registered trademark of **American Express Company**.

Once your score increases, allow your most recent account to age on your credit reports at least 12 months before applying for new credit. Before applying for a new car or mortgage loan, get pre-approved through a credit union. Shopping for new credit products without being pre-approved is a recipe for disaster and may result in too many inquiries or denials.

Credit Tip:
When shopping for a new car or mortgage loan, inquiries captured within 14 days typically count as <u>one</u> inquiry.

Breaking Down Your FICO®[11] Scores

Most lenders and banks use FICO scores. With over ten variations of FICO scores and new versions introduced annually, it's essential to know the scores lenders use when approving you for different types of credit. In this section, I'll cover the most commonly used FICO scores and what to do if denied for these types of credit.

FICO Mortgage Scores:

Your mortgage credit scores are calculated using your payment history, debt-to-income ratio, and credit utilization. Mortgage lenders use your FICO mortgage scores to approve or deny your mortgage application. Your FICO mortgage scores are Experian[12] FICO Score 2, TransUnion[13] FICO Score 4, and Equifax[14] FICO Score 5.

---

[11] FICO is a registered trademark of the Fair Isaac Corporation: https://www.fico.com/.
[12] Experian is a registered trademark of Experian Inc.: https://www.experian.com/.
[13] TransUnion is a registered Trademark of TransUnion, Inc.: https://www.transunion.com/.
[14] Equifax is a registered trademark of Equifax: https://www.equifax.com/.

Here are a few reasons why you may be denied a mortgage loan:

- Your credit card balances or debt-to-income ratio is probably too high;
- You have recent delinquency, such as late payments, new collection accounts, or repossessions;
- You have a recent bankruptcy.

Getting pre-approved doesn't automatically guarantee your final loan application will be approved. You can still be denied once the loan enters underwriting and the lender examines your financial profile more closely. The Equal Credit Opportunity Act says a lender has 60 days to provide you, in writing, with specific reasons why your loan application was denied. If you are denied a mortgage due to a lack of credit history, you should take steps to build your credit.

FICO Auto Scores

Auto financing companies use similar FICO scores as mortgage lenders to calculate your FICO auto scores. Your FICO auto loan scores are Experian FICO Scores 2 or 8, TransUnion FICO Scores 4 or 8, and Equifax FICO Scores 5 or 8. Financing companies review your credit reports to determine if you can make timely auto loan payments. Existing late payments can cause you to be approved with conditions, which means receiving a higher interest rate, paying a higher down payment, or being denied. Like mortgage loans, your FICO auto score relies heavily on your debt-to-income ratio. If your outstanding balances on installment loans or credit cards are too high, financing companies could deem you a risk and stick you with an excessive interest rate.

FICO Credit Card Scores

If you've ever applied for a credit card and received a credit decision that says, "We'll send you a decision within 7-10 business days," more than likely, your application was denied. In rare instances, you may be asked to provide more information to verify your identity. Companies like Chase®[15] have the unspoken "5/24 rule." The 5/24 rule is the unofficial rule that claims Chase won't approve you for its cards if you've opened five or more personal credit card accounts from any issuer in the last 24 months. Similarly, American Express will not approve you for its credit products if you have too many inquiries, high balances, recent delinquency, or late payments. This is not an official rule of the company but has been the experience based on current Chase and Amex credit card holders and applicants.

Here are some of the top reasons you were denied a credit card:

- Your loan or credit card balances are too high.
- You have too many inquiries.
- Your income is too low.
- You have too many credit cards.
- You have a recent collection or public record (tax lien, bankruptcy, etc.).
- You were recently late on an account, or your last delinquency was too recent.
- You have a recent charge-off on your credit report.
- You have a credit history that is too short.
- You didn't submit the correct information in the application.

---

[15] "Chase," "JPMorgan," and "JPMorgan Chase" are trademarks of JPMorgan Chase Bank, N. A

PART II

NAVIGATING YOUR CREDIT REPORTS

STEP ONE

PULLING YOUR CREDIT REPORTS

B efore I get into the first step of the guide, as I mentioned in the introduction, it is designed to be followed to ensure optimal results. Skipping over steps will not yield positive results.

This may seem obvious, but the first step to fixing your credit is downloading a copy of your most recent credit reports from Equifax, Experian, and TransUnion. Information on your credit reports changes often. What may have been reported on your credit report last month may not be the same as today. You'll also want to request copies of your credit reports from credit reporting agencies that influence credit decisions, like Innovis Credit Report and LexisNexis. Download multiple copies of your credit reports at the beginning of each month to monitor your reports for changes and updates. You are also entitled to free copies of your credit reports directly from the credit bureaus and can request these copies both in writing and online.

If you were recently denied new credit, you are entitled to a copy of your credit report and a summary of why you were denied. This is known as an adverse action notice. If you receive an adverse action notice after being denied credit, this letter will describe how your credit profile prevented you from obtaining new credit, employment, or housing. The information in this notice can be used to repair your credit.

To help you get started, I've partnered with Credit Dyno to give you exclusive access to monthly credit monitoring at an affordable price. With Credit Dyno, you can access your credit scores and reports from any device. Plus, you get real-time alerts to monitor and stay on top of changes to your accounts and credit scores, including fraud alerts. Visit https://tinyurl.com/creditdyno to sign up for credit monitoring with Credit Dyno.

The Primary Credit Bureaus

Experian
P.O. BOX 4500
Allen, Texas 75013
www.experian.com

Equifax Information Services
P.O. Box 740256
Atlanta, GA 30374
www.equifax.com

TransUnion Consumer Solutions
P.O. Box 2000
Chester, PA 19016
www.transunion.com

Innovis Consumer Assistance
P.O Box 53088
Atlanta, GA 30353
www.innovis.com

Other Credit Reporting Agencies

There are over two hundred specialty credit reporting agencies that play a role in whether financial institutions extend you new credit. These credit reporting agencies provide information to companies about your credit history when you apply for employment, apartments, car insurance, bank accounts, etc. While they are not responsible for approving or denying your credit applications, the information in these reports can positively or negatively impact whether your application is fully approved, approved with conditions, or if you'll have to pay higher deposits than someone with better credit.

Here are the primary credit reporting agencies that store your financial information:

ChexSystems, Certegy, Telecheck, and E.W.S. (Early Warning Systems) - These companies provide information related to your checking and savings account history to banks when you apply for new bank accounts. Certegy and Telecheck also verify check transactions electronically to prevent check fraud. E.W.S. is jointly co-owned by Bank of America, BB&T, Capital One, JPMorgan Chase, P.N.C. Bank, U.S. Bank, and Wells Fargo and exchanges information across bank partners.

LexisNexis – LexisNexis maintains information about public records like judgments, tax liens, or bankruptcies. The credit bureaus often use LexisNexis to verify public records since the court doesn't report directly to the bureaus. LexisNexis is also used to perform identity verifications.

CoreLogic – CoreLogic collects and reports data related to property ownership and home loan obligation records, property legal filings, tax payment status, rental applications, and collection accounts. They also maintain information about consumer bankruptcies, liens, judgments, and outstanding child support obligations.

C.L.U.E Auto (Comprehensive, Loss Underwriting, Exchange) – C.L.U.E is a database that maintains your auto and insurance claims information when you apply for home or auto policies.

The National Consumer Telecom & Utilities Exchange – The NCTUE is a collection of companies that maintain information about your payment history with phone, utility (electric, gas, or water), and cable providers.

Tenant Screening Agencies – Tenant Screening agencies like Experian Rent Bureau and Rent Grow maintain information about your rental history and evictions.

Like the credit bureaus, the credit reporting agencies are <u>REQUIRED</u> to follow the FCRA in ensuring the information in these third-party reports is accurate. You can request free copies of your consumer reports from these agencies annually. Before applying for new credit, the rule of thumb is to always "know before you go." Your credit reports and scores should never be a surprise to you.

The Consumer Finance Protection Bureau (CFPB) compiles an annual list of the specialty credit reporting agencies. For the most up-to-date list, go to the CFPB website and click on "Consumer Reporting Companies."

> **Credit Tip:**
>
> The bottom line is that any time you apply for a job, apartment, bank account, or car, there is a credit reporting agency that provides your information to those lenders.

STEP TWO

BREAKING DOWN YOUR ACCOUNTS

Not knowing how to read your credit reports properly can cause you to miss serious violations. Finding these violations is critical in helping you remove inaccurate, unverifiable, and outdated information from your credit reports. These errors can also cost you credit denials, money, or both. Resolving these errors will help you improve and increase your credit scores.

Your credit reports are divided into four **main sections:**

1. Personal Information;
2. Account History;
3. Public Records; and
4. Inquiries.

Your credit report **does not** contain the following:

1. Your salary information;
2. Your bank account information;
3. Your credit score - unless the report is purchased through a third-party reseller;
4. Your spouse's information - unless you have a joint account, or they cosigned for credit on your behalf; or
5. Utility Bills – unless they were sent to a collection company.

Personal Information

The personal information section of your report includes your name, date of birth, social security numbers, addresses, phone numbers, and employers that have been reported to the credit bureaus through your creditors. This section often contains minor errors; although innocent, these errors could be a sign of identity theft. Monitor your personal information closely and keep it updated annually.

The personal information reporting on your credit reports **needs to** be accurate. Disputing old addresses, names, and employers is your right. Many people use one address for everything - usually a parent's address. This is a bad idea. You should not have no more than TWO addresses listed on your credit reports since (1) lenders may use this as a red flag while reviewing your mortgage application, and (2) collection agencies will use your outdated personal information to verify if an alleged collection account belongs to you.

Credit bureaus like Experian use address identifier numbers to connect your address to your account information. This information is provided through your creditors and the U.S. Postal Service when you initiate a change of address. Before you send your initial dispute letter to the credit bureaus or debt collectors, make sure your personal information is corrected or updated. This is a critical step that helps you maximize your dispute results. Since the credit bureaus verify all disputes electronically, they simply use the information in your credit to prove ownership. Without removing outdated personal information, it makes it easier for the credit bureaus to verify your dispute without even investigating.

While reviewing your personal information, check for these errors:

1. Misspelled or Duplicate names
2. Outdated or Incorrect addresses
3. Wrong Date of Birth
4. Incorrect Social Security Number
5. Incorrect Employer Names
6. Inaccurate Phone Numbers
7. Any personal information that does not belong to you

Reviewing Personal Information

Review your personal information from your credit reports and list all incorrect information in the box below. Use the questions below to audit your personal information:

1. Are there names you do not recognize?
2. Are there other dates of birth?
3. Is your Social Security Number correct?
4. Are there incorrect or old addresses listed?
5. Is your phone number correct?

6. Do you want your phone number listed? (You can request to have your phone number removed from your credit report)

List the personal information that needs to be corrected:

Names	Date of Births	Social Security Numbers	Addresses	Phone Numbers

Account History

The account history section of your credit report is one of the most important sections because it contains information about how you manage your accounts. This is where most of the errors are included in your credit reports. The two main types of accounts are "Credit Accounts" and "Collection Accounts."

Credit Accounts

Credit accounts are the positive or negative accounts reported directly by your lenders.

These accounts will list the following:

- Lender's Name
- Partial Account Number
- Date Opened
- Account Type
- Date of Last Payment
- Date Last Reported
- Date of Last Activity
- Amount Owed
- Pay Status (current or late)
- Credit Limit
- High Credit
- Payment History

Collection Accounts

Collection accounts result in accounts sold to a collection agency by the original creditor or another collection agency.

These accounts will list the following:

- Agency Name
- Partial Account Number
- Date Opened
- Account Type
- Date of Last Payment
- Date Last Reported
- Amount Owed

Sometimes, collection accounts may list the original creditor's name, but occasionally, you will need to contact the collection agency to receive this. Don't be afraid to get the information you need. You can use the collection agency script in the tools and resources section to learn how to effectively communicate with debt collectors.

While reviewing account information, check for these types of errors:

- Outdated account information (Delinquent accounts reported after seven years and six months);
- Incorrect account numbers;
- Accounts that have been re-aged;
- Incorrect Account balance;
- Wrong Account opening date;

- Incorrect credit limit;
- Credit card account not reporting credit limit;
- Incorrect account type;
- Charge-off that has been sold or transferred with a past due balance instead of zero balance;
- Charge-off account showing currently past due,
- Open charge-off accounts;
- Accounts that are not included in bankruptcy;
- Collection accounts with a credit limit;
- Closed accounts reported as open;
- An account where you are reported as the primary owner instead of an authorized user;
- Accounts incorrectly reported as late or delinquent,
- Accounts with a wrong date of last payment, date opened, or date of first delinquency;
- Accounts with the same debt listed more than once (possibly with different names or different companies;
- Account not belonging to you with a similar name (Your credit report may be merged if your name is similar or the same as someone else);
- Reinsertion of incorrect information after it was corrected;
- Accounts that appear multiple times with different creditors listed (especially in the case of delinquent accounts or accounts in collections); and
- Accounts not belonging to you due to identity theft

Credit Tip:

With collection accounts, it's important to verify the date of delinquency, also known as the first time the account is late or delinquent. Some collection agencies often try "account re-aging" as a scare tactic to get you to pay the account before validating it. When this happens, the account may appear on your credit report longer, often decreasing your credit score. This is underline illegal, and you should immediately report this to the FTC and CFPB.

List Your Negative Accounts Here:

Creditor	Account Number	Date of Last Payment	Balance

Public Records

The public records section contains financial data from accounts such as bankruptcies, judgments, and tax liens. It does not contain information related to arrests or criminal convictions. The National Consumer Assistance Plan, established in 2017, mandated that Credit Bureaus could only report public records if sufficient personally identifiable information existed on the records AND if the records were updated at least every 90 days. To be reported accurately, public records must include complete name, full date of birth and/or social security number, and address. The Credit Bureaus removed most public records like tax liens and civil judgments as of 2018 due to non-compliance with this law.

LexisNexis is the primary company that provides information about your public records to the credit bureaus. Before disputing public records with the credit bureaus, you can dispute these accounts directly with LexisNexis. Remember, the information reported by LexisNexis must be reported accurately and be verifiable.

While reviewing your Public Records, check for these errors:

1. Public record data not verified every 90 days by the data furnisher.
2. Public record data that does not contain, at a minimum, name, address, social security number, and/or date of birth.
3. Debts not arising from a contract or agreement to pay (think library late fees, parking tickets, etc) can no longer appear on credit reports.

Inquiries

Inquiries are divided into two types: hard inquiries and soft inquiries. Hard Inquiries are obtained by applying for new credit. When you apply for credit, prospective lenders will pull your credit reports to evaluate your creditworthiness. A lender <u>MUST</u> have your permission and a permissible purpose to pull your credit file for a hard inquiry. Inquiries can remain on your reports for 25 months. After 12 months, they no longer damage your scores; after six months, they minimally affect them. You should only dispute inquiries less than one year old and not attached to open accounts. Disputing inquiries attached to open accounts can inadvertently close the account and flag the account as fraud.

Soft inquiries can come from three sources: when you access copies of your credit reports or scores, when existing lenders review your credit, or when companies "pre-approve" you for potential credit offers. Soft inquiries have no impact on your credit scores. If you have an open account with a creditor, they may periodically check your credit to offer you more credit cards, increase your credit line, or reduce your available credit. An example of a company that monitors your credit reports is American Express. When they periodically review your credit and notice your score has declined, or your credit card balances are too high, they may reduce your credit limit on the open credit cards you have with them.

While reviewing your inquiries, check for these errors:

1. A hard inquiry from a company you have never applied to.
2. A hard inquiry without your permission.

3. An inquiry resulting from identity theft.
4. Inquiries are listed after 25 months from the date of application.

Reviewing Inquiries:

Review your credit report and list all inquiries under 12 months old. ONLY dispute inquiries that you don't have accounts for. For example, if you have a Capital One account, you can't dispute the inquiry you received when you opened that account.

Creditors	Date Reported

PART III
OPERATION DISPUTING

DISPUTING YOUR ACCOUNTS

N ow that you understand your rights, have thoroughly reviewed your credit report errors, and know what goes into building your credit scores, it's time to dispute the errors in your accounts. As previously stated, you should remove outdated or incorrect addresses before disputing negative accounts so the credit bureaus don't automatically verify negative accounts.

Next, dispute any collection accounts directly with the credit bureaus first. Remember, the credit bureaus and credit reporting agencies must ensure that the information in your credit profile is verifiable, accurate, and timely. The bureaus typically have 30-45 days to respond to your request, so during this time, send a similar letter directly to the creditor or collection agency.

In part three, I'll review the step-by-step process for repairing, rebuilding, and restoring your credit and easy-to-use dispute templates to achieve diy credit mastery. These are just templates, so adjust the wording based on your tone of voice for best results.

STEP THREE

UPDATING YOUR PERSONAL INFORMATION

U se the templates on the following pages to correct your personal information. The timeline below advises the best time to mail your letters, where to mail them, and what letter(s) to send if you don't get a prompt response.

What to Send:	To	When:
Letter #1	Main Credit Bureaus, LexisNexis, and Innovis	Day 1
If the credit bureaus respond to Letter #1 indicating that correcting addresses associated with accounts on your reports should be updated by the original creditor, this is not true. In this case, send Letter #2.		
Letter #2	Main Credit Bureaus	When letter #1 does not result in removal

Letter #1 - Personal Information Letter

Your Name
Your Address

Credit Bureau
Bureau's Address

Date

To Whom This May Concern:

I have noticed concerning items under the consumer information section of my credit reports. Please update my personal information. I have provided all of my creditors with my correct personal information. If they report anything else, it violates FCRA requirements, which require reporting true and accurate information. Since you are also required to ensure this information is true and accurate, you are required to correct this information.

Please correct my personal information to ONLY what is reflected below and delete any erroneous information:

Name: Jane Doe
DOB - 01-02-03
SSN: 123-45-6789
Address: 123 My Street Name, NC 12345

Please know that I do not want my telephone numbers to be listed. Please correct this information immediately and send me an updated copy of my report to the above address.

Your Printed Name - Do not hand-sign

Enc: Copy of License, Social Security Card

(Include a copy of your utility bill if the address on your license does not match)

Letter #2 - Personal Information Letter - No Response

Your Name

Your Address

Credit Bureau

Bureau's Address

Date

To Whom This May Concern:

On (insert date), I requested that your agency update and correct my personal information on my credit report. It is both the creditors' responsibility and yours to report only true and accurate information.

I have provided all of my creditors with my correct personal information. If they report anything else, it violates FCRA requirements, which require reporting true and accurate information. Since you are also required to ensure this information is true and accurate, you are required to correct this information. Therefore, I demand that you delete the erroneous information from my file.

Further, the erroneous information below is still listed on my report, and since you are required to report only true and accurate information, this will be my final request for you to correct this. If the actions are not completed within 30 days, I will file a complaint and possibly initiate legal action. Please delete the following information:

1)

2)

3)

I look forward to your response. Please include a copy of my updated report to reflect your changes.

Your Printed Name - Do not hand-sign
Enc: Copy of License, Social Security Card

(Include a copy of your utility bill if the address on your license does not match)

STEP FOUR

HOW TO DISPUTE INQUIRIES

U se the templates on the following pages to dispute inquiries. The timeline below advises of the best time to mail your letters, where to mail them, and what letter(s)to send if you don't get a timely response.

What to Send:	To	When:
Letter #3	Credit Bureau	Day 1
Letter #4	Creditors	When letter #3 does not result in removal
Letter #5	Credit Bureau	At the same time, you send #4
Letter #6	Creditors	If Letter #4 does not result in removal

Letter #3 - Inquiry Removal Letter

Your Name

Your Address

Credit Bureau

Bureau's Address

Date

To Whom This May Concern:

I recently applied for credit, and one of the reasons I was denied was due to the number of inquiries on my report. I reviewed my credit file and am disturbed by the number of inquiries I do not recognize.

I do not recognize the following inquiries:

- Name of Company and Date of Inquiry
- Name of Company and Date of Inquiry

Under the FCRA, you can only report true and accurate information. Since inquiries must have a permissible purpose and an agreement signed by me, I ask you to remove the erroneous inquiries.

Without proper verification provided to me within 30 days of receiving this letter, you must remove the unverifiable information from my file. Also, since I have been denied credit in the last 60 days, you must also provide me with a copy of my credit report. Please also provide this in your response.

Please provide me with the following information for each inquiry listed:

- Permissible purpose;
- Verification of permission to inquire - bearing my signature;
- Name of the person at your company who verified with the creditor; and,
- Name of the person at the creditor's company who provided the information.

I appreciate you taking the time to send me this information, and I will be in touch after receiving your response.

Your Printed Name - Do not hand-sign
Enc: Copy of License, Social Security Card

(Include a copy of your utility bill if the address on your license does not match)

Letter #4 - Inquiry Removal Letter

Your Name
Your Address

Creditor's Name
Creditor's Address

Date

To Whom This May Concern:

I recently reviewed my credit file, and I am disturbed by the inquiry from your company. I am trying to remember when I authorized you to pull my credit file. According to my credit file, you placed an inquiry on (insert date).

Under the FCRA, you can only report true and accurate information. Inquiries must have a permissible purpose and an agreement signed by me giving permission to view my report. Therefore, please prove that you were authorized to pull my credit report. Without verification provided to me within 30 days of receiving this letter, you must remove the information from my file.

Please provide me with the following information regarding your inquiry:

- Permissible purpose; and
- Verification of permission to inquire - bearing my signature.

If you cannot provide this information within 30 days, I request that you immediately remove the inquiry from my credit file. I appreciate the time you will take to send me this information, and I will be in touch once I receive your response.

Have a fantastic day!

Your Printed Name - Do not hand-sign
Enc: Copy of License

Letter #5 - Inquiry Removal Letter

Your Name
Your Address

Credit Bureau
Bureau's Address

Date

To Whom This May Concern:

Thank you for responding to my letter on (insert date) regarding the erroneous inquiry reporting on my credit report from your company. Under the FCRA, you can only report true and accurate information. Inquiries must have a permissible purpose and an agreement signed by me giving permission to view my reports.

Since you have yet to provide me with the requested information or have yet to do so within the 30 days legally allotted to you, I demand that you immediately remove the inquiry from my file.

You have 15 days to respond to this letter informing me that you plan to remove the inquiry from my file. If by the 15th day, I have yet to hear from you, I will file complaints with the Consumer Financial Protection Bureau, the Federal Commission, and the Attorney General's Office. Do not underestimate my knowledge of my rights. This is a simple mistake with a simple resolution on your end.

I appreciate you taking the time to send me this information, and I will be in touch after receiving your response.

Your Printed Name - Do not hand-sign

Enc: Copy of License, Social Security Card

(Include a copy of your utility bill if the address on your license does not match)

Letter #6 - Inquiry Removal Letter

Your Name
Your Address

Creditor's Name
Creditor's Address

Date

To Whom This May Concern:

Thank you for responding to my letter on (insert date) regarding the erroneous inquiry reporting on my credit report from your company.

Under the FCRA, you can only report true and accurate information. Inquiries must have a permissible purpose and an agreement signed by me giving permission to view my report. Therefore, I asked you to provide competent evidence that you were authorized.

Since you have not provided me with the requested information or have not done so within the 30 days legally allotted, I demand that you immediately remove the inquiry from my file.

You have 15 days to respond to this letter informing me that you plan to remove the inquiry from my file. If by the 15th day, I have not heard from you, I will file complaints with the Consumer Financial Protection Bureau, the Federal Commission, and the Attorney General's Office. Do not underestimate my knowledge of my rights. This is a simple mistake with a simple resolution on your end.

I appreciate you taking the time to send me this information, and I will be in touch after receiving your response.

Your Printed Name - Do not hand-sign

(Include a copy of your utility bill if the address on your license does not match)

STEP FIVE

UPDATING LATE PAYMENTS

When disputing late payments, first, write down any late payments reported within the past 18 months and verify them against your bank statements to ensure they were late. If you were, in fact, late, request a goodwill adjustment. When requesting a goodwill adjustment it's a good idea to pay off high credit balances before requesting a goodwill adjustment. This will increase your score VERY quickly. I've gotten great results when removing late payments by sending goodwill letters to the company's CEO directly. You can get this information by visiting ceomail.com. Goodwill requests are not guaranteed, even when contacting the company's CEO.

When disputing late payments, ensure you are not requesting that the entire account be removed or deleted. Removing an established account with only a few late payments can severely impact your credit score, causing you to lose the positive payment history associated with this account. When disputing late payments, always request that the credit bureau and creditors mark the account as "Paid As Agreed or Never Late." If you have more than two late payments reporting, only dispute two to three late payments per letter to increase the chances of late payments being removed.

Use the templates on the next few pages to dispute late payments. The timeline below advises of the best time to mail your letters, where to mail them, and what letter(s)to send if you don't get a timely response.

What to Send:	To	What Letter:
Letter #7	Data furnisher/ creditor	Request transaction history
Letter #8	Data furnisher/ creditor	Goodwill Request letter

Letter #7 – Request Transaction History

Your Name

Your Address

Creditor's Name

Creditor's Address

Date

To Whom This May Concern:

I recently reviewed my credit report and found inaccurate and incomplete information. You are reporting late payments on the following dates:

- insert date of late payment
- insert date of late payment

These dates do not match my records, and the notation of the following late payments is inaccurate. Please investigate and verify that all data for this account is reported accurately, including every notation, date, and balance, whether reported or not.

Please send me a copy of my transaction history from (insert date three months before alleged late payment) to (the current date), including all statements and payment transaction records from the creditor that would prove that my payment was not submitted on time. If you can't provide me with the transaction history, please update these payments to show on time and paid as agreed. I under-stand that if you are required to report true and accurate infor-mation but can't validate it, you must update or remove it.

I appreciate the time you will take to investigate this, and I will look forward to your response within 30 days.

Your Printed Name - Do not hand-sign

Letter #8 - Goodwill Request Letter

Your Name
Your Address

Company Name
CEO of Company (You can find this on CEOmail.com)
CEO Email Address

Date

To Whom This May Concern:

I noticed that my most recent credit report contains a late payment(s) reported on [insert date(s)] for my [insert company name] account. I understand and have great respect for my financial obligations. Unfortunately, at the time of the incident mentioned above, I had [insert circumstance that caused you to miss a payment – hospital stay/injury/job loss/etc.].

Aside from these unforeseen and unavoidable circumstances, you will see that I have an excellent payment record. I plan on applying for [insert plan on how you'll be using for credit, i.e., mortgage/auto loan/etc.], and it has come to my attention that the missed payment(s) on my credit reports could hurt my ability to qualify.

Please know the missed payment doesn't reflect my creditworthiness and commitment to repaying my debts. I humbly ask you to give me a second chance by making a goodwill adjustment to the late payment on [insert date(s)] from my credit reports. As I understand it, you can do so in just a few minutes of your time. I would greatly appreciate it!

In exchange, I signed up for autopay to decrease the chances of being late again! Thank you for your consideration.

Have a blessed day!
Your Printed Name - Do not hand-sign

STEP SIX

SLASHING CREDIT CARD DEBT

Your credit utilization substantially impacts your credit score: 30%, to be exact. As mentioned earlier, credit utilization is how much of your available credit limits are used. The higher that percentage, the more significant the negative impact on your score. To prevent your utilization from damaging your score, keep your credit card balance below or around 10% of your available credit. To build your credit, you should keep your monthly balances under 5-10%, with the ideal balances being 1-2%. It's important that you use the cards regularly to show responsibility for using credit.

Creating a Budget To Slash Debt

Paying off credit card debt is a marathon, not a sprint. This is an area in which I had to become disciplined since I would find myself "stress spending." This is also one of the fastest methods to improve your credit scores in a short time. Believe it or not, the answer to your spending problems is NOT more credit cards. Do not get sucked into applying for more credit because your credit scores are increasing. Focus on building 12 months of consistent discipline with the cards you already have. If you are repairing your credit and don't have credit cards, I added links to some of my favorite credit builder cards in the tools and resources section of the guide.

The Zero-Based Budget

Zero-based budgeting is my favorite budgeting method. This budget method gives every cent of your money a specific purpose down to zero. For example, if you make $5000 a month and pay $2,000 for rent, you will allocate $2,000 for rent and assign $3,000 to other expenses, including savings and investments, until you've reached zero; hence "zero-based." Creating a zero-based budget lets you track where and how your money is spent. This reduces the chances of you overspending and increasing your debt.

The 50/30/20 Budget

Another budgeting method is the 50/30/20 budget. This method splits your monthly income into three categories: 50% of your **after-tax** income goes toward required expenses like housing, car payments, and groceries. 30% is used for your wants like hair, nails, and shopping, and 20% for savings and retirement.

The Debt Avalanche Method

The debt avalanche method is a savings strategy to pay off debt according to the highest interest rates. For example, if you have four credit cards, identify the card with the highest interest rate and pay this account off, putting extra money towards the balance to prevent compound interest from increasing your monthly payments. If you get paid bi-weekly, it may be a good idea to pay on this account twice a month until it is paid in full. Remember, your payment will only be reported to the credit bureaus once a month.

Ensure you still make minimum payments on your other credit card accounts. You'll repeat this cycle until your debt is paid in full.

The Debt Snowball Method

The Debt snowball method is a popular method where you'll make minimum payments on all debts — except the smallest one. With this method, you'll attack the smallest debt with any extra money you have. This includes money freed up from budgeting or adding a side hustle. Once the smallest debt is paid off, add the amount you were paying to that debt to the next card's monthly payment. Continue this method until you've paid off your debt. For example, let's say you have three credit cards, make the minimum payment, and add $40 to the balance. If the monthly payment of your lowest credit card balance is $100, add an extra $40 to the monthly payment each month until the credit card is paid in full. After the first credit card balance is paid off, you'll take $140 and add it to the monthly payment of the second credit card. So, if you already paid $150 monthly towards the second credit card, you'll now pay $290 monthly.

Thrift Savings Plan[16]

You've probably heard of the Thrift Savings Plan or TSP, which is a retirement savings and investment plan designed specifically for federal employees, including members of the military. But, you may not be taking full advantage of a TSP account's pre-tax and retirement benefits.

One of the primary advantages of opening a TSP account is the tax-deferred contributions, which allow servicemembers to reduce the taxes they must pay while saving for retirement. The TSP offers a range of low-cost investment options, providing servicemembers the opportunity to build a diversified portfolio tailored to their risk tolerance and financial goals. Additionally, the TSP allows you to make automatic monthly contributions directly from your military pay, simplifying the savings process and promoting financial discipline.

The TSP offers two options for diversifying your retirement and investing portfolio: the Traditional Plan and the Roth Plan. The traditional plan provides service members the opportunity for compound growth over time, as earnings on contributions accrue, tax-deferred, until withdrawn. Even if you finish your contract term or decide to end your military service, the TSP allows for portability, allowing servicemembers to continue managing their retirement savings, even if they transition to civilian employment. With a Roth TSP, your contributions go into the TSP after tax withholding. That means you pay taxes on your contributions at your current income

---

[16] Thrift Savings Plan is a registered trademark of TSP Services Inc (2015)

tax rate. The advantage of the Roth TSP is that you won't pay taxes later when you take out your contributions and any qualified earnings.

Using your Thrift Savings Plan offers a secure and tax-efficient way for service members to build a solid financial foundation for retirement. For 2023, the annual limit for TSP contributions was $22,500, plus $7,500 if you're 50 or older for both Traditional and Roth. For 2024, the yearly limit of regular TSP contributions is $23,000.

You may also be eligible for a loan through TSP with your contributions. However, the loan may be subject to fees, penalties, and interest. For more information on how to navigate your Thrift Savings Plan, visit https://www.tsp.gov/tsp-basics/

"MONEY IS QUEEN BUT CREDIT IS KING"

STEP SEVEN

REBUILDING YOUR CREDIT HISTORY

T o build credit and establish a healthy credit mix, you need at least five open and positive reporting accounts on your credit reports. Again, since payment history is 35% of your credit score, the more accounts you have with a good payment history, the better your score. Believe it or not, you must have open credit cards to build credit. You may be someone who doesn't like using credit cards due to a lack of discipline–or you'd rather not deal with the stress of managing them–but they are still needed to build credit.

If your credit scores are below 600, you're less likely to be approved for unsecured credit cards. These cards are based solely on your credit scores and payment history and do not require collateral or a deposit. No matter how many offers you receive, do not apply for unsecured credit cards while fixing your credit. This will avoid unnecessary inquiries and decrease scores. Instead, opt for a secured credit card with no credit check. Check out my credit builder secured credit card if you need an affordable secured card option. I recommend this card to all my clients, building credit during the repair process. Apply for the credit builder card here: https://www.creditbuildercard.com/cierramichelle.

To establish a healthy credit profile, ensure you have the following mix of accounts:

- 3 Revolving accounts, including secured or unsecured credit cards.
- 2 Installment accounts, including student loans, car loans, mortgages, self-lender, and personal loans.

Authorized User Accounts, also called Tradelines

Most credit card companies allow authorized users to be added to a credit card. The primary account holder's payment history and credit utilization will reflect on the authorized user's credit reports. When someone is added as an authorized user, this is sometimes called credit piggybacking. Unless you are the primary user's direct relative, I don't recommend purchasing a tradeline or an authorized user account from someone you don't know.

Credit Privacy Numbers, or CPNs, have gained popularity recently. Using illegal tradelines acquired without permission from the primary account holder or opening lines of credit using a CPN is illegal. Attempting to apply for a mortgage loan using a CPN is a federal offense and is considered mortgage fraud, which carries a potential penalty of 30 years in federal prison.

STEP EIGHT

OPERATION DISPUTING

N ow, it's time to start disputing your accounts with the credit bureaus. The three credit bureaus use an electronic verification system called E-Oscar to process disputes. This system often results in disputes being automatically verified that are not compliant with FCRA standards and are unreliable at best. You can use this to leverage disputing unverifiable information on your credit reports. Do not send in handwritten letters. You want the system to read your written disputes accurately.

Use the addresses below to send your dispute letters:

The Primary Credit Bureaus

Experian

P.O. BOX 4500

Allen, Texas 75013

www.experian.com

Equifax Information Services

P.O. Box 740256

Atlanta, GA 30374

www.equifax.com

TransUnion Consumer Solutions

P.O. Box 2000

Chester, PA 19016

www.transunion.com

Innovis Consumer Assistance

P.O Box 53088

Atlanta, GA 30353

www.innovis.com

The Initial Dispute Process

The first dispute letter will only list the first five derogatory accounts. Limiting your disputes to five accounts every 14 days will make the credit bureaus more likely to reject your disputes and mark them as frivolous. Track the dates your letters are mailed by sending your disputes via certified mail to maximize your results. This way, when your certified receipt is returned, you can compare the date on the return notice with the postmarked date of your letter. The FCRA gives the credit bureaus 30 days from receipt of your dispute letter to complete the investigation. They may receive an additional 15 days, for a total of 45 days if - and ONLY if - you mailed additional information regarding the dispute AFTER the initial dispute letter was received.

Use the suggested timeline in the table below to mail your disputes:

What to Send	What Accounts	When
Letter #9	First five accounts	Day 1
Letter #9	Next five accounts	Day 14
Letter #9	Next five accounts	Day 21

Letter #9 - Initial Dispute Letter

Your Name
Your Address

Credit Bureau
Bureau's Address

Date

To Whom This May Concern:

I recently looked at my credit report, and I am unable to match the debt(s) below to any debt(s) I am aware of. Please verify these accounts to help clarify why these debts are reported on my credit reports.

Below is a list of the information in my report:

1. (Creditor Name) claims I owe (amount) and was last reported on (date) under account number (insert number including the ****)
2. (Creditor Name) claims I owe (amount) and was last reported on (date) under account number (insert number including the ****)

If you cannot verify the information for the above accounts, I demand that the accounts be removed immediately. I have attached a copy of my license, social security card, and utility bill to prove my identity and residence. These are acceptable forms, according to your website.

Thank you for your prompt attention to this matter. I look forward to getting this resolved as soon as possible. I will expect your response in less than 30 days.

Warm Regards

Your Printed Name - Do not hand-sign
Your Social Security Number

PS. I am keeping a careful record of all correspondence with you in case you fail to verify these accounts, and legal action is required.

Responding To Stall Letters from The Credit Bureaus

Sometimes, when the credit bureaus become aware that you are trying to fix your credit, they will send what are known as stall letters to slow down your progress. They do this to get you to stop your credit repair journey because they think the average consumer does not know their rights. In my years of fixing my credit and working with veterans, I've seen my fair share of stall letters.

Here are some examples of stall tactics used by the Credit Bureaus:

- They claim your investigation is frivolous.
- They claim you didn't send the required proof of ID.
- They claim they could not locate your credit file with your provided information.
- They claim you did not write the letter or that you're working with a credit repair company - this is why using YOUR tone of voice in the templates is important.

If you get a stall response, use one of the letter templates below based on the bureau's response to your dispute.

What to Send:	Letter Type:
Letter #10	Not Enough ID
Letter #11	Cannot Locate File
Letter #12	They Do Not Believe It Was You
Letter #13	Frivolous Investigation

Letter #10 - Not Enough ID

Your Name
Your Address

Credit Bureau
Credit Bureau's Address

Date

To Whom This May Concern:

I mailed a letter on (insert date) asking you to investigate accounts on my credit reports. I have attached a copy of my previous letter with the exact proofs of ID and residence I originally sent. Additionally, I included a copy of your response, claiming I needed to send the correct identifying information, along with documentation from your website proving the proper information was sent.

I know you are aware of the laws, so I won't include them in this letter, but you only have 30 days to investigate my disputes. Since I sent the correct information and you attempted to manipulate me by stating I did not, you only have until (30 days from today's date) to finish investigating my dispute. I am distraught that you would try to get over on me as if I am an uneducated consumer.

I am looking forward to receiving the results of the requested investigation. This erroneous information is damaging my credit.

Warm Regards,
Your Printed Name - Do not hand-sign
Enc: Copy of License, Social Security Card

PS. I am keeping a careful record of all correspondence with you in case you fail to verify these accounts, and legal action is required.

(Include a copy of your utility bill if the address on your license does not match)

Letter #11 - Cannot Locate File

Your Name
Your Address

Credit Bureau
Bureau's Address

Date

To Whom This May Concern:

I wrote a letter on (insert date) asking you to investigate a few accounts. I have attached that letter with the exact proofs of ID and residence I originally sent. You responded, claiming you could not locate a file with my provided information. You're trying to stop my investigation request even though I provided you with the correct information. I am rewriting my personal information again for you in large letters so you can read it correctly.

- MY NAME IS (INSERT),
- MY ADDRESS IS (INSERT) AND
- MY SOCIAL SECURITY NUMBER IS (INSERT).

I know you are aware of the laws, so I won't include them in this letter, but you only have 30 days to investigate my disputes. Since I sent the correct information and you attempted to manipulate me by stating I did not, you only have until (30 days from today's date) to finish investigating my dispute. I am distraught that you would try to get over on me as if I am an uneducated consumer.

I am looking forward to receiving the results of the investigation I requested. This erroneous information on my credit report is damaging my credit through no fault of my own.

Warm Regards,
Your Printed Name - Do not hand-sign
Enc: Copy of License, Social Security Card

PS. I am keeping a careful record of all correspondence with you in case you fail to verify these accounts, and legal action is required.

(Include a copy of your utility bill if the address on your license does not match)

Letter #12 - They Do Not Believe It Was You

Your Name
Your Address

Credit Bureau
Credit Bureau's Address

Date

To Whom This May Concern:

I sent a letter on (insert date) requesting you to investigate the accounts. I have attached this letter with the exact proofs of ID and residence I originally sent. You responded with claims that someone else wrote the letter. Why would someone write a letter inquiring about lousy information in my report? That's just stupid, and I believe you're trying to stall my investigation. Whether or not you think I wrote this letter doesn't matter. I provided my signature (no one else can do that) and proved my identity with the proper documents, as indicated on your website.

How would you expect me to verify my identity? It's not like I can send you a DNA sample. Please complete my investigation and cut out the elementary behavior.

I know you are aware of the laws, so I won't include them in this letter, but you only have 30 days to investigate my disputes. Since I sent the correct information and you attempted to manipulate me by stating I did not, you only have until (30 days from today's date) to finish investigating my dispute. I am distraught that you would try to get over on me as if I am an uneducated consumer.

I am looking forward to receiving the results of the investigation I requested. This erroneous information on my credit report is damaging my credit through no fault of my own. Please be advised that if you continue to stall or refuse to investigate, I am prepared to file a complaint with the Consumer Financial Protection Bureau and initiate a small claims suit.

Warm Regards
Your Printed Name - Do not hand-sign

PS. I am keeping a careful record of all correspondence with you in case you fail to verify these accounts, and legal action is required.

(Include a copy of your utility bill if the address on your license does not match)

Letter #13 - Frivolous Investigation

Your Name
Your Address

Credit Bureau
Credit Bureau's Address

Date

To Whom This May Concern:

I sent a letter to you on (insert date) asking you to investigate a few accounts. I have attached that letter with the exact proofs of ID and residence I originally sent. You responded, claiming you believe the investigation requests are frivolous. What gives you the right to decide that? This consumer report is about me, and under the laws, I have EVERY right to dispute information I do not recognize.

I don't know what makes you believe you have the legal right to deny my investigations, but I can and will exercise my rights under the law to file complaints against you with the Consumer Financial Protection Bureau. I will also file a small claims lawsuit against you if you continue to deny my request for investigation, as is my right under the FCRA.

I know you are aware of the laws, so I won't include them in this letter, but you only have 30 days to investigate my disputes. Since I sent the correct information and you attempted to manipulate me by stating I did not, you only have until (30 days from today's date) to finish investigating my dispute. I am distraught that you would try to get over on me as if I am an uneducated consumer.

I am looking forward to receiving the results of the investigation I requested. This erroneous information on my credit report is damaging my credit through no fault of my own.

Please be advised that if you continue to stall or refuse to investigate, I am prepared to file a complaint with the Consumer Financial Protection Bureau and initiate a small claims suit.

Warm Regards
Your Printed Name - Do not hand-sign

PS. I am keeping a careful record of all correspondence with you in case you fail to verify these accounts, and legal action is required.

(Include a copy of your utility bill if the address on your license does not match)

If The Bureaus Fail to Respond to Your Dispute Request

You should receive a response from the credit bureaus within 30 days. By day 45, if you have not received a response, the credit bureaus have violated your rights under the Fair Credit Reporting Act, and you can hold them responsible. When this happens, send another letter via certified mail requesting that the accounts included in your disputes be removed, updated, or corrected since they have failed to respond within the 30-day timeline. Only allow them 30 more days to do so, and remind them it's your right and intention to escalate this claim should they refuse to comply.

If the credit bureaus respond that the account was verified as accurate and belongs to you, you can request the credit bureau's Method of Verification or MOV. Under FCRA Section 611 (a)(6) and (7), you have a right to request their method of verification, and they only have 15 days to respond to this request. A method of verification request is making the credit bureaus prove how they reached their investigation results. A MOV template is available in letter #14 of the template index of this section. If they do not respond to the MOV request within this timeframe, file a complaint with the Consumer Financial Protection Bureau via their website, www.consumerfinance.gov, upload proof of your correspondence, and mail letter #15 to the credit bureaus via certified mail.

As you receive written responses from the credit bureaus, refresh your credit reports via Credit Dyno to monitor for changes. Remember, you can only refresh your credit reports once every 30 days, so if you refresh before your disputes are complete, you'll have to wait another month to view new reports.

If the Bureaus Still Fail to Remove the Account

As a disclaimer, I am not an attorney, so this is NOT legal advice. If you are still waiting to receive responses from the credit bureaus, I recommend hiring a consumer protection attorney or purchasing a low-cost Legal Shield subscription. By ignoring your request, the credit bureaus have willfully violated your rights, and you may be entitled to compensation should you decide to sue. Again, I am not an attorney, so please contact an attorney to pursue this matter through the proper channels.

What to Send	What Accounts	When
Letter #14	First 5 accounts	Within 5 days of receiving a response
Letter #15	Next 5 accounts	Within 5 days of receiving a response
Letter #15	Next 5 accounts	Within 5 days of receiving a response

Letter #14 - Method of Verification

Your Name
Your Address

Credit Bureau
Credit Bureau's Address

Date

To Whom This May Concern:

On (insert date), I wrote a letter asking you to investigate inaccurate accounts on my credit reports. I have attached my previous letter to confirm the date it was written. On (insert date), you responded that the account was verified, but I am sure this account needs to be (insert desired result - corrected or deleted) (on/from my credit report).

I am now exercising my rights under FCRA 611(a) (7) to request a complete description of all methods used to investigate my dispute. Please include a copy of all correspondence and contact information for each company, along with the names of the employees who helped verify the information.

If you cannot provide me with these details within the 15 days you're allowed to do so, I demand you remove the accounts from my credit report. Failure to do so can and will result in legal action. Do not underestimate my knowledge of my rights.

Warm Regards,
Your Printed Name - Do not hand-sign

Letter #15 - Failure of MOV Process

Your Name
Your Address

Credit Bureau
Credit Bureau's Address

Date

To Whom This May Concern:

I wrote a letter to you on (insert date) requesting your agency investigate erroneously reporting accounts. You responded on (insert date) that the account was verified. When I asked for a description of your procedures on (insert date), you either failed to respond timely or did not provide the requested information.

At this point, I am agitated that your agency has ignored me, treated me like an uneducated consumer, and caused my family and me great distress. Leaving negative information on my credit file has prevented me from (insert your situation, for example: buying a house, renting an apartment, purchasing a new car, etc.), which is unfair to me and my family.

Attached are copies of all my letters on this matter, including your responses and complaints submitted to the Consumer Financial Protection Bureau, the Federal Trade Commission, the Better Business Bureau, and the Attorney General.

I am no longer asking but demanding that you remove the accounts you failed to verify. If you ignore my rights, I intend to initiate a court action. I have carefully documented all my correspondence with you and will present it to the court.

We can avoid this and resolve the complaints if you follow the law and remove these accounts. I will give you ten days to do so.

I look forward to your quick response.

Warm Regards
Your Printed Name - Do not hand-sign

STEP NINE

CRUSHING THE CREDITORS

N ow that you understand how the dispute process works when disputing directly with the credit bureaus, I will show you how to dispute directly with your creditors or collection agencies.

Disputing directly with the creditors can be both beneficial and effective. The dispute process for creditors, including collection agencies, begins with debt validation. While waiting for results, start the debt validation process with the creditor or collection agencies. The requirements for debt validation under the FDCPA are vague, but in a courtroom, a judge would require proper and undeniable evidence that the debt belongs to you. The burden of proof is on the creditors, not the consumers. Therefore, you can have an erroneous account removed from your credit report by forcing the data furnishers to provide the same court-barred evidence.

Some collections agencies may respond with a copy of a bill, but anyone can open an account under your name for which a bill is produced, so this doesn't mean the account belongs to you or that the debt is yours. Make creditors provide factual evidence. This evidence consists of a contract from the original creditor or a document bearing your signature agreeing to pay the debt. In the absence of this evidence, it is unlikely that the court will rule in the collections agency's favor, so it is fair to request that the account be removed from your credit report. The creditors and collection agencies must mark the account as disputed on your credit reports within 30 days of receipt of your letter. Check your credit report on the 31st day and print it with a timestamp. If it was not reported as disputed, they must remove it.

Credit Tip:

If the letter comes back undelivered, send a copy to the bureau, and they will remove the account due to the creditor not reporting true and accurate information regarding their business.

What to Send	What Letter	When
Letter #16	Debt Validation Letter	At the same time, you send MOV to the bureau on this account
Letter #17	If they respond without a contract	Within 5 days of receiving their letter
Letter #18	If they do not respond after 30 days	Within 5 days of receiving their letter
Letter #19	If they respond again without a contract	Within 5 days of receiving their letter

Letter #16 – Debt Validation Letter

Your Name
Your Address

Creditor/Collection Agency's Name
Creditor/Collection Agency's Address

Date

To Whom This May Concern:

I recently viewed my credit reports after being denied credit, and I am concerned about finding an account reporting incorrectly by your company. When speaking with my neighbor, I learned that this violates my rights, and I would like to know why you intend to hurt me by reporting erroneous information.

This letter is regarding (insert account number). I would like to be sent evidence that this account belongs to me. Please note that I will not accept a copy of a bill as evidence. I am asking you to send court-worthy proof that verifies the debt belongs to me, such as a contract bearing my signature.

Without this evidence, the debt you claim I owe is invalid. If you cannot prove that I agreed to pay this debt, I request that you immediately remove the report from my credit file.

I know you are aware of the laws, so I won't include what I read online, and I know you will do your due diligence to uphold the regulations in the FDCPA and FCRA. I am recording correspondences via certified mail should I seek legal relief. I expect your response within 30 days.

Thank you for your time and attention to the matter.

Warm Regards
Your Printed Name - Do not hand-sign

Letter #17 - Response Without Proof

Your Name
Your Address

Creditor/Collection Agency's Name
Creditor/Collection Agency's Address

Date

To Whom This May Concern:

In response to your letter on (insert date), you still claim that I allegedly owe (insert amount) on account # (insert number). You did not provide the evidence I requested, so how was this account validated without proof that I agreed to pay this debt?

Please provide me with a description of your company's validation procedure, the name of the employee, and a phone number so I can inquire about how the account was validated. Again, you have not provided me with validation, and I am upset that you continue to violate my rights. I know you know the laws, so I don't have to remind you that you're breaking the FCRA and FDCPA by reporting unverifiable and invalid information. Even worse, you're STILL doing so after I requested validation, which you failed to provide.

I am suffering financial distress due to your actions, and my anxiety has reached its limit. I am no longer asking but demanding you remove the item from my credit file. This is the last time you will be reminded of your responsibilities. Your follow-up letter should let me know you are removing the account from my credit file and ceasing further collection activity.

Let me remind you that your 30 days to provide the requested debt validation have passed, and since you have failed to do so, you're now required by law to remove the account from my credit file.

I am keeping careful correspondence logs in case I need to seek judicial relief.

Warm Regards
Your Name - Do not hand-sign

Letter #18 - No Response Within 30 Days

Your Name
Your Address

Creditor/Collection Agency's Name
Creditor/Collection Agency's Address

Date

To Whom This May Concern:

I wrote you a letter on (insert date) requesting validation on the following account:

- Account Name and Account Number:
- Amount Owed

You have failed to respond to my letter, which I have tracked as arriving on (insert date) within the 30 days that the law gives you to respond. You are in violation and under the remedies of the regulation. You now must remove the account from my credit file.

You only have 15 days to remove the above account before I file a small claims lawsuit against you. I am confident I will win since I have sustained the burden of proof. It would be financially beneficial to you to quickly remove the account than face the amounts I am entitled to under the FDCPA.

I look forward to your response.

Warm Regards
Your Printed Name - Do not hand-sign

Letter #19 - Second Response and Intent to File Suit

Your Name
Your Address

Creditor/Collection Agency's Name
Creditor/Collection Agency's Address

Date
To Whom This May Concern:

Throughout our correspondence, it has become clear to me that you do not care about my rights as a consumer or the laws that protect me from predatory practices. I have meticulously recorded my correspondence, and I am confident that a judge will rule in my favor.

As such, I have filed a small claims lawsuit against you, and you are now required to appear at:

(Insert Court Name and Address)
On: (Insert Date) to answer to the following claims:

- Violations of the Fair Credit Reporting Act
- Violations of the Fair Debt Collection Practice Act
- Defamation of Character
- Violations of [insert any corresponding state laws if you desire]

I am seeking (insert amount) in damages. If you correct your records and delete the information between now and the above court date, please contact me at the address listed above, and I will withdraw the claim immediately.

I look forward to your quick response.

Warm Regards
Your Printed Name - Do not hand-sign

(Only send this letter if you have contacted a consumer protection attorney or legal representative. Do not threaten a company with actions you don't intend to take.)

STEP TEN

SETTLING ACCOUNTS WITH CREDITORS

Unfortunately, even with the best dispute strategies, disputing an account won't always result in removing the account from your report. If you have disputed using every method possible and the creditors sent you the required documentation, you can request to settle the account. However, before accepting defeat, make sure you have diligently followed the dispute process. During my journey, I've had to dispute accounts as many as five times before they were removed or corrected on my reports.

Creditors and collection agencies usually want to recoup whatever they can. Often, they rather receive a partial payment than no payment at all, so they will often settle for less than what you owe. This settlement strategy can help even if you have already paid off an account. It also works if you want to settle an account in exchange for removal or to lessen the impact on your score.

The first step is to write a letter requesting a settlement. Be careful not to make the initial offer because you may over offer. Your request should be an emotional plea but a stern reminder that if you "consider" filing for bankruptcy, they get nothing; therefore, it's in their best interest to settle. If their first offer is unreasonably high, respond in writing and remind them that due to your current financial obligations, you cannot pay above 50% but will be willing to pay between 30% and 50% of the total balance. The object of the game is to settle lower than the original offer.

It's essential to request settlements in writing. Sometimes, debt collectors will respond to your request via phone to try and collect the remaining balance with a verbal agreement. Maintain your stance, and let them know any communication regarding the debt needs to be done in writing. Save all written correspondence once the creditors or collection agency agree to settle. If they attempt to rescind their offer or collect on the remaining debt outside of the parameters of the agreement, then they have breached the settlement. Also, ensure the settlement agreement prohibits the resale of the remaining debt. If you can't get a lower offer, request a conditional acceptance offer.

To request a conditional acceptance offer, write a letter stating that you will accept the settlement in exchange for the following.

- 3-6 months to pay;
- Removal of the debt from your report upon satisfactory payment and
- The creditor/collection agency agrees not to resell the remaining debt balance.

- A signed letter by a person of authority confirming the agreement will be mailed to you before making your first payment.

Once you receive the signed contract or a letter acknowledging the agreement terms, make your payments as agreed.

CONGRATULATIONS, YOU DID IT!

———

Throw the confetti and pop the champagne! You have successfully achieved credit mastery. Don't worry if you didn't get the results you wanted the first time; remember, it may take a few rinses and repeat cycles. Still need help or have questions? Visit my website, cierramichelle.com, for more DIY resources like courses, eBooks, and masterclasses to help you rebuild and repair your credit. I hope you enjoyed this guide, and if so, please share it with a fellow veteran and leave a five-star review on our Amazon book page.

PART IV

MISSION ACCOMPLISHED

BONUS RESOURCES

CREDIT REPAIR RESOURCES

Credit Dyno

highly recommend (and love) using CreditDyno.com to monitor my credit reports for updates. Credit Dyno lets you seamlessly pull all three credit reports. Credit monitoring services help you stay on top of any changes or suspicious activity on your credit report, which can help prevent identity theft and fraud. Additionally, Credit Dyno can alert you to potential errors on your credit report and help you improve your credit score over time.

Visit https://tinyurl.com/creditdyno to begin monitoring your credit.

Dispute Beast

Dispute Beast is an AI-powered Credit repair software that lets you effortlessly create dispute letters for negative accounts in less than

15 minutes. I've partnered with Dispute Beast to give you exclusive access for FREE when you sign up for Beast Credit Monitoring.

Visit this link https://disputebeast.com/partner/creditcoachcierra/ to get started with Dispute Beast.

Credit Builder Resources

Below are some of my favorite credit builder resources. These recommendations are great for establishing credit. Some product links may be affiliate links. If you click on any of the links and purchase within a specific timeframe, I'll earn a small commission. The commission is paid by retailers at no cost to you.

Capital One Affiliate Link

I love my cards from Capital One. Their pre-approval tool makes it easy to see what cards you're eligible for without impacting your credit score. Plus, no credit score is required to apply. Want to check it out? Visit this link to find the card that's right for you! https://capital.one/3JQpBlx

Credit Builder Card from Credit Coach Cierra

The Credit Builder Card is a secured credit card that reports your positive payment history to all three credit bureaus to help raise your credit scores. Learn more about the credit builder card here: https://www.creditbuildercard.com/cierramichelle.

Self-Lender Affiliate Link

Using Self's credit builder account can help you increase your credit scores by up to 49 points. Self Lender reports to all three credit bureaus, typically within 72 hours of opening a new account. Plus, building with Self Lender means you get access to Self's Secured Visa Credit card in as little as three months with no credit check. Visit https://self.inc/refer/16608965 to get started.

Money Saving Resources

You can't make money moves that make "cents" without having a savings plan.

Before you put this book down, open an account using one of these resources and establish a savings account for travel, sinking funds - which are created for planned variable expenses like hair, nails, shopping, etc. - and emergency funds, which you should aim to save a minimum of six months of your total expenses.

Here are a few of my favorite savings accounts.

High Yield Savings with Ally.

One of my favorite savings accounts is through Ally Financial. Ally is a high-yield savings account that allows you to organize your savings goals into "buckets." Visit ally.com to get started.

High-yield Savings with Capital One.

Capital One is also a high-yield savings option with comparative rates and no monthly or maintenance fees—what you earn is what you keep. Visit capitalone.com to get started.

Start Investing with Fidelity.

Got stock? Fidelity makes it easy to start investing with a free brokerage account. I contribute $50 per month to my Fidelity account, where I can transfer the dividends from stocks to build my 401K Roth, giving me double the tax benefits. Visit fidelity.com to get started.

Collection Agency Script[17]

What To Do When a Debt Collector Calls

The first call with a debt collector can be stressful because it can catch you off-guard. If you get a call from a debt collector, first determine who they are and which debt they are collecting. Then, end the call and verify those details. Here are some other common steps to take in a debt collection call:

Decide if you want to talk now. Remember that you are in control of the conversation, not the debt collector. If it's not a good time to talk, ask them to call you back. That way, you can develop a strategy and avoid making costly mistakes.

---

[17] Learn more on how to communicate with debt collectors by visiting https://www.the-balancemoney.com/what-to-

Be sure to only confirm your name. Debt collectors can't go into any details until they know it's you they're speaking to. If you don't confirm your name, you can't get any information.

Don't provide any more details. Just because someone calls you and knows your personal details doesn't mean it's a legitimate call. Don't provide personal details outside your name. Do not provide your social. Often, debt collectors will ask for your last four. Respond by saying if you are trying to collect an alleged debt from me, please send me a debt validation letter within five business days of this phone call.

Ask for details about your debt. Not all debts are real, especially if there was a reporting error or someone stole your identity. Ask about the debt amount and the original creditor, then reach out to the original creditor to confirm that it's a real debt and that they handed it off to the collection agency.

End the call to check the information. Let the debt collector know you'll need to verify the details on your own before proceeding. Don't agree to make any payments, and don't provide any more information.

Determine an action plan. If it's a fake debt, contact the FTC and consider reporting it to local authorities. If the debt is legitimate, make sure it's not past the statute of limitations. From there, you can decide whether and how to work with the debt collector to pay it off, including whether you want to hire an attorney.

Remember, paid collections are NOT automatically deleted from your credit reports. You can negotiate their removal using the methods in step ten.

Credit Scores Tracker

Use the tracker below to track your scores each month.
Pay close attention to significant changes to your scores.

Month	Experian	TransUnion	Equifax

ABOUT THE AUTHOR
Cierra Michelle Jones

Cierra Michelle Jones, MBA, is a U.S. Army Veteran and a Certified Credit Coach. As the creator of DIY Credit Mastery, she teaches you how to repair, rebuild, and restore your credit the legal way. Cierra coaches veterans and consumers on leveraging strategic credit habits for homeownership. She advocates for military programs such as V.A. Loans to build generational wealth. Learn more at CierraMichelle.com

www.ingramcontent.com/pod-product-compliance
Lightning Source LLC
Chambersburg PA
CBHW071427210326
41597CB00020B/3693